THE
S.C.R.I.P.T

An Armor of Hope Manual
for Aspiring Christian Authors

This Journal Belongs to:

_____

Scripture taken from the New King James Version®. Copyright © 1982 by Thomas Nelson. Used by permission. All rights reserved.

Printed in the United States of America

First Printing, 2018

All rights reserved.

Armor of Hope Writing & Publishing Services, LLC.

WEBSITE OR SOCIAL MEDIA INFO:
www.armorofhopewritingservices.com
www.denisemwalker.com
armorofhope121@gmail.com

ISBN:978-0-692-16932-2

THE S.C.R.I.P.T

AN ARMOR OF HOPE WRITING JOURNEY

The **S.C.R.I.P.T.** *is an acronym created by me, Author Denise M. Walker, owner of Armor of Hope Writing & Publishing Services and founder of Hope-in-Christ Ministries. God placed this method in my spirit as I began to write my own books to draw others to Christ.*

S.C.R.I.P.T. *is a tool that will keep you focused on your why. Writing is a ministry, and our relationship with Him helps us to truly understand our purpose for why we do what we do.*

Script *will keep you on the right track.*

I will walk you through getting started with your writing career.

In the first section, we will take a look at a few scriptures regarding God's purpose for our lives. Keep these scriptures before you as you go forward.

In the second section, we will walk through each component of the **S.C.R.I.P.T.** *and apply them to writing with a purpose.*

Finally, we will deal with the logistics of writing and the tools needed to assist you in your writing success.

"We have to stop trying to write our own script and allow God to show us the one that's already written."
— Owner/Author/Chief Editor
Denise M. Walker

Table of Contents

Section 1:

God's Word, Our Foundation

Scripture:

"But seek first the kingdom of God and His righteousness, and all these things shall be added to you." – (Matthew 6:33)

This is one of my favorite scriptures. It tells us that God has to be first in our lives. He is life. Therefore, we must seek Him for our purpose.

In the Strong's Bible Dictionary, seek means to aim at, strive after, or seek for.

During my short time in the literary arena, I have witnessed individuals focused on the wrong things: money, status, or recognition. As Christian writers, we *must maintain focus on God's purpose for our journey, souls. To do this, we must stay close to God. He has all we need.*

How will this scripture help you on your writing journey?

Respond to the question(s) here:

_____

_____

_____

_____

_____

_____

_____

_____

_____

_____

_____

_____

_____

Scripture:

"And do not be conformed to this world, but be transformed by the renewing of your mind, that you may prove what is that good and acceptable and perfect will of God."
- (Romans 12:2)

The word that stands out here is **conform**. It means to change your mind and character and be like someone else.

Why is not conforming to the world's way as a writer so important?

Why is our transformation so critical here?

How will you get rid of any stinking thinking that you may have acquired along the way?

Respond to the question(s) here:

Scripture:

"Before I formed you in the womb I knew you; Before you were born I sanctified you; I ordained you a prophet to the nations."

(Jeremiah 1:5)

This scripture reminds us that we are more than flesh and our purpose is deeper than we can imagine. God knows more about us than we know about ourselves. He's the designer of our being and has purposed us to tell others about Him.

Why is this scripture important to your writing journey?

Respond to the question(s) here:

_____

_____

_____

_____

_____

_____

_____

_____

_____

_____

_____

_____

_____

_____

_____

_____

_____

Scripture:

"And we know that all things work together for good to those who love God, to those who are the called according to His purpose." – (*Romans 8:28*)

There are some things from our past that can hinder our current or future successes. In order to walk in our full purpose, we have to deal with these issues upfront.

I had to take off fear, abuse, rejection and so much more before ever moving forward with my writing. Otherwise, I may have been writing with a spirit of unforgiveness or retaliation. This is not God's will.

We can't assist anyone else until we allow God to take us through the healing and deliverance process.
What are some of the things you need to give to God?

Respond to the question(s) here:

_____

_____

_____

_____

_____

_____

_____

_____

_____

_____

_____

_____

_____

_____

Scripture:

"Your word is a lamp to my feet
And a light to my path." –
(Psalm 119:105)

This scripture reminds us of how important God's instructions are to our success in life. You may be thinking of one kind of success. However, I am referring to a successful God-fearing, purposed filled life.

How will God's word be used as a lamp and light? How will you keep from going the wrong way? A way that God didn't direct you.

Respond to the question(s) here:

_____

_____

_____

_____

_____

_____

_____

_____

_____

_____

_____

_____

_____

_____

_____

_____

_____

_____

_____

_____

_____

Scripture:

"There are many plans in a man's heart, Nevertheless the Lord's counsel—that will stand." (Proverbs 19:21)

This is our final scripture of focus before moving into the steps of writing.

Place your plans for writing before God. Ask His direction before starting. Remember, no matter how slow or fast paced your journey is, listen for His direction and purpose in it.

How does this final scripture speak to you?

Think of an individual that will hold you to this scripture. Who are they? List them below. Ask them if they wouldn't mind being your spiritual mentor.

Respond to the question(s) here:

_____

_____

_____

_____

_____

_____

_____

_____

_____

_____

_____

_____

_____

_____

_____

Section 2:

The S.C.R.I.P.T. Explained

What is my success?

God created each of us to be successful in our own area and not someone else's. It is important that we understand this at the beginning to help push us forward in what God has called us to be.

Here is a hint: There is something that you are very passionate about and you don't stress out at all about it.

What skills, gifts, or talents did you acquire previously that will flow into your writing journey?

25

Ex: I have taught English for many years. My target audience has been middle grades students. This is the group that God led me to minster to through my writing, but now He's stretching me using the same gifts.

Respond to question(s) here:

_____

_____

_____

_____

_____

_____

_____

_____

_____

_____

_____

What is my Capacity?

Capacity – *This part is how much you think you can handle as a writer. This must be identified so that you can pray for God to send assistance or tools for the areas needed.*

Are you technology driven?

Can you draw or design?

Do you have some gaps in writing? Grammar? Punctuation? Structure?

Add as needed.

Respond to the question(s) here:

_____

_____

_____

_____

_____

_____

_____

_____

_____

_____

_____

_____

_____

What is my Role?

Here you will think about the role you will play in your writing career. Your role in your writing success is very important.

When I say success, I am referring to your longevity in the literary industry. Our writing career should never be focused on money. We are called to minister to others through our literature. Therefore, God will bring the increase. Focus on the why factor.

How will you set aside time with God for prayer and Bible study so that you can receive His guidance?

What training or workshops would you like to invest in?

How will you hold yourself accountable to get your writing done and not make excuses?

How will you minimize distractions and separate yourself to put your best foot forward?

Respond to the question(s) here:

_____

_____

_____

_____

_____

_____

_____

_____

What is my True Identity?

We have to keep in mind what God said about us. If you don't, it will hinder your writing journey. You will assist others in knowing who they are through your writing. Therefore, you must know who you are in Christ. He gives us the power to take off the falsehood and walk in truth. He did it for me; he will do the same for you.

What things may hinder you from fully walking in God's truth about you?

Also, there are many authors and genres out there. However, God has gifted you and I with an individuality which no one else has. We have to believe that with all of our heart.

Don't get distracted, side tracked or develop envy regarding how anyone else is walking in their purpose.

What is your unique overall vision for your writing ministry?

What theme is God showing you?

Respond to question(s) here:

_____

_____

_____

_____

_____

_____

_____

_____

What is my Purpose?

What do you want highlighted, or what are you advocating?

How will it help the audience?

What other plans do you have to expand your ministry beyond your book?

Respond to the question(s) here:

_____

_____

_____

_____

_____

_____

_____

_____

_____

_____

_____

_____

_____

_____

_____

_____

_____

_____

_____

_____

What is my Territory?

What specific territory do you want to cover through your writing ministry?

Do you want to reach schools, government offices, churches, or individuals?

Do you want it to be local, state, or international?

How do you plan to do this?

Respond to the questions here:

Section 3:

The Logistics

Logistics 1: Genre

Now that we have looked at the purpose for why God has called us to write, we will go over a few logistics to help you get started.

What is your genre (poetry, fiction, non-fiction, autobiography)?

How will you write it? (first person or third person)

Why do you want to use this method?

Respond to question(s) here:

_____

_____

_____

_____

_____

_____

_____

_____

_____

_____

_____

_____

_____

_____

_____

_____

_____

_____

Logistics 2: Theme

Theme – lessons or morals

What theme or lesson(s) do you want in your book?

How will the genre that you chose fit with the theme you have chosen?

How do you want to structure your book (chapters, days, weeks)?

Respond to the question(s) here:

_____

_____

_____

_____

_____

_____

_____

_____

_____

_____

_____

_____

_____

_____

_____

_____

Logistics 3: Plan

Now it's time to plan your writing. There are different strategies for different genres.

Non-fiction
Chapter titles/themes
Don't make it too long. Consider breaking into two books if needed.
Organize your chapters.
Be careful not to repeat information.

Fiction

Write out a plot for your story ahead of time.
Develop the scenes.
Think ahead as you develop the characters.
Pay attention to your transitions that relate to time.
Be sure not to leave the reader wondering.
Make sure your vocabulary matches your audience.
Don't make mistakes with the names.

Poetry

This should flow as the gift that God has given you.
Use rhyming patterns.
Create Stanzas.
Organize your poems by theme.

Write out a plan on the lines on the pages that follow.
It does not have to be perfect, but you must have a plan.

Respond to the question(s) here:

Logistics 4: Get it Written

Now that you have your plan and your layout, let's get to writing.

Don't talk yourself out of this victory. Procrastination could be motivated by fear. Don't worry about how it sounds. Just write.

On the next page, start your first chapter (theme) or opening to your story.

Identify areas where can you add more details.

Example: *(Non-Fiction) My childhood struggles began when I was only four years old.*
(Fiction) Elizabeth rushed into her office unaware of what she would face that day.

First Chapter:

_____

_____

_____

_____

_____

_____

_____

_____

_____

_____

_____

_____

_____

Logistics: Revisions

After finishing your first chapter, follow these steps and again once you finish your first draft.

Take out any repeated parts or unessential information.

Add specific details where needed.

Decide if you need to move around sections or paragraphs.

Make sure you have a sequential order.

Listen to your book.
Sometimes you can't hear repeated parts or confusing sections until you listen to the words. There is a tool at the end of the book that is great.

Reference any Scriptures.

Reference anything that you took from some where else.

Add pronouns where you have repeated names over and over.

Make sure you haven't used "and" over and over.

Add chapter titles.

Determine if it is too long or too short.

Make sure you haven't used others' names without permission.

Use synonyms for repeated words.

Notes:

Grammar Tip 1

Sometimes we repeat without realizing it. If you have said that same thing two different ways, take out the repeated part and **elaborate** on the thought.

When you **elaborate**, you tell more or start answering the who, what, when, where, why and how questions.

Take a sentence from your opening and **elaborate** on the lines provided.

Notes:

Grammar Tip 2

Do *not* use **double negatives**.

Double negatives can easily be a hang up for us if we are not careful. One example of a double negative is the following:

I **didn't** have **nothing**. This may sound simple enough, but this is an error I see often while editing. Pay attention to this and make a quick fix.

Correction: I **didn't** have **anything.**
Practice writing a few in your notes section. Double check your manuscript for any used.

Notes:

Grammar Tip 3

*Watch your sentence structure. Try to **avoid run-ons**.*

You don't have to be a grammar scholar, but this part is very important. The editor will make the final corrections for you, but sentence structure is important. This helps you to better hear the flow of your writing before sending it to the editor.

At the end of every thought, add a period, exclamation, or question mark.

Don't overuse the conjunction "and" when trying to combine thoughts.

Combine sentences *that relate in thought to avoid choppy sentences.*

Example:
Leslie ran to grab a bite to eat. She went to the pharmacy.

Combined: *Leslie ran to grab a bite to eat, and she stopped by the pharmacy.*

On the way home, Leslie ran by the pharmacy and grabbed a bite to eat.

Error:
Leslie ran and grabbed food and went to the pharmacy. (Overuse of the conjunction "and")

Practice combining a few of your sentences from your first chapter in the notes section.

Notes:

83

Grammar Tip 4

Watch your subject/verb agreement.

Subject/Verb agreement can also trip us up while writing. Try to make sure they are correct as you write. Remember, if the nouns are more than one, the verb should be "were or are." If the nouns are singular, the verb should be "was" or "is."

Example:

Error: They **was** going to the mall.
Correction: They **were** going to the mall.

Error: They **is** friends.

Correction: They **are** *friends.*

Create a few examples in your notes if this is an area of concern for you.

Notes:

_____

_____

_____

_____

_____

_____

_____

_____

_____

_____

_____

_____

_____

Grammar Tip 5

Remain in the same tense throughout your manuscript.

Verb tense *is another common error I find while editing. Remember, whatever tense you begin with, you must continue writing in that same tense. Therefore, your manuscript shouldn't contain verbs with "ing" and "ed" at the same time. Choose one or the other.*

Past Tense (Already happened) – Most Verbs end in "ed"

Present Tense (Currently happening) - Most Verbs end in "ing."

Future Tense (Has not yet happened) – Verbs start with "will"

Note: *Past or Present tense are commonly used while writing.*

Notes:

_____

_____

_____

_____

_____

_____

_____

_____

_____

_____

_____

_____

_____

_____

_____

_____

Grammar Tip 6

Watch your dialogue.

Dialogue *is not only used in fiction writing. It can also be used in poetry and non-fiction. When using dialogue, be sure to punctuate correctly. Also, if your tags repeat, use synonyms for those words.*

Said - replied, stated, responded

Error:
She said "Come by the shop tomorrow".
Correction:
She said, "Come by the shop tomorrow."

Error:
"Meet me at the office" monet stated.

Correction:
"Meet me at the office," Monet stated.

Correction:
"Meet me at the office." Leslie stated cheerfully.

Notes:

_____

_____

_____

_____

_____

_____

_____

_____

_____

_____

_____

Reflections:

_____
_____
_____
_____
_____
_____
_____
_____
_____
_____
_____
_____
_____
_____
_____
_____
_____
_____
_____
_____
_____

Tools to Use

1. **Voice Dream Reader App** – use to listen to your manuscript
2. **Merriam Webster Dictionary and Thesaurus** – use to correct spelling, look up definitions, and add synonyms
3. **Amazon** – Amazon often has free ebooks related to writing. Check it often.
4. **Writing groups** – Join online writing groups in your genre.
5. **Blogs** – Search for writing blogs. They often provide great tips.
6. **Pinterest** – Start a Pinterest account. It contains a wealth of information.
7. **Create Social Media pages** – Create an Instagram, Twitter, Facebook and LinkedIn author page. Start sharing about your book ahead of time.
8. **Amazon Author Page** – Create an Amazon Author page where you can add more information about yourself.
9. **The Christian Writers Institute** – They offer refresher courses for a reasonable price.
10. **Voice recording app** – Find an app that you can use to gather your thoughts when your away from home.

11. **Plot-generator.org.uk** – This is a great tool. It generates random story ideas.
12. **Grammar Girl** – This is a great resource. She has a podcast, blog and books to refresh your grammar skills.
13. **Bowker Identifier Services** – This is the official site for purchasing your ISBN number. https://www.myidentifiers.com/my_company
14. **Copyright.gov** – This is the official site for submitting your manuscript to receive your copyright number.
15. **Hope-in-Christ Book Club** – This is my online ministry. You can join as a Christian author. We fellowship, share important information, collaborate, hold interviews and offer services to one another.
16. **The Scribes' Network** – This is a new group that I am starting as a part of my coaching. This is an accountability group that will meet monthly online and in person. I will hold the members accountable for getting their vision completed. You do not have to be a coaching client to be a part of this network. Contact: armorofhope121@gmail.com if you would like to join.

17. **Self-Publishing Platforms** – *Createspace, Ingram Spark and Lulu

ABOUT THE AUTHOR

Denise M. Walker is a wife and mother. She is a minister, entrepreneur, and educator.

Denise has educated youth for almost 20 years. Most of her career has been teaching English language arts to middle school students. She is the founder of Hope-in-Christ Ministries and the owner of Armor of Hope Writing & Publishing Services.

Denise is the creator and facilitator of the Hope-in-Christ Book Club Facebook group and is the host of two ministry podcasts. Her ministry's mission is to lead others to their true identity in Christ and allow Him to be the center of their life.

Through Armor of Hope, Denise is the chief editor, literacy builder, curriculum writer and writing coach. Denise seeks to bring hope to others and help them bring forth God's vision.

www.ingramcontent.com/pod-product-compliance
Lightning Source LLC
Chambersburg PA
CBHW050540280326
41933CB00011B/1664